JOURNEY INTO SPACE

PREVIOUS BOOKS BY SEÁN STREET

Poetry

Figure in a Landscape
A Walk in Winter
This True Making
Radio and Other Poems
Time Between Tides
Cello
Jazz Time
Camera Obscura
The Sound Recordist

Prose

The Wreck of the Deutschland
The Dymock Poets
The Poetry of Radio
The Memory of Sound
Sound Poetics
Sound on the Edge of Perception
The Sound inside the Silence
The Sound of a Room
Wild Track

JOURNEY INTO SPACE

SEÁN STREET

Shoestring Press

Printed by imprintdigital
Upton Pyne, Exeter
www.digital.imprint.co.uk

Typesetting and cover design by The Book Typesetters
us@thebooktypesetters.com
07422 598 168
www.thebooktypesetters.com

Published by Shoestring Press
19 Devonshire Avenue, Beeston, Nottingham, NG9 1BS
(0115) 925 1827
www.shoestringpress.co.uk

First published 2022
© Copyright: Seán Street
Cover painting: Cuckmere Haven, 1939 (pencil & w/c on paper) – Eric Ravilious, (1903–42) © Towner Collection. Towner Gallery, Eastbourne / Bridgeman Images

The moral right of the author has been asserted.

ISBN 978-1-912524-87-7

ACKNOWLEDGEMENTS

Some of these poems, or previous versions of them, have been published in the following:

Acumen, Agenda, Creative Flight, The Honest Ulsterman, Lapwing Press, The Manhattan Review, Poetry Birmingham, The Poetry Society's *Poetry News, Raceme, Scintilla, Tears in the Fence* and *The Rialto.* 'Formby Beach' was written as a response to a commission by the BBC Radio 4 programme, *Front Row* for National Poetry Day, 2018. Thanks to the BBC Radio producer, Julian May. Gratitude is due to the editors who facilitated the first publication of some of the poems: Matthew Barton, Sheri Benning, David Caddy, Philip Fried, Danielle Hope, Michael Mackmin, Gregory McCartney, Patricia McCarthy, Patricia Oxley and Joseph Sterrett.

For Jo, Jemma, Zoë and Phoebe

CONTENTS

NOTE TO SELF

To cherish: both a learnt skill and a gift
like seeing by looking, listening by hearing,
like healing, the sweet art of noticing
as circumstances dance, as shadows shift.

To learn it isn't hard, doesn't take long.
Found intuitively or consciously,
nurtured in the everyday carefully,
it doesn't take long. But there isn't long.

SWIMMER

Me, ten, water-phobic,
pale and beached as he aimed
himself like Leander
out a straight mile from shore,
heading toward something
it seemed only he saw,
vanishing into it
and swallowed between waves'
unremitting horizons.

Then the seed of his head
safe in shallows, his laughter
as he strode up shingle.
But these were childhood times
before there were endings,
when he always came back.
And look now, the nothing
he swam away to all
those years ago. Still there.

BLACKTHORN, CELANDINE

To name is to invoke
root, flower, fruit –
the space around them,
Blackthorn, Celandine –
the shapes leaf and word,
tree and poem, make.
To say is to see them:
plant, word, spring-water clear.

ISLANDNESS

Joe Heaney

Be a teller of songs, a singer
of tales, a match for the liminal,
the islandness of it weathered
by the spit and taste of the mouth's salt,

because it's the salt coast makes us sing
against tide, a noise to drown sea-wash
at a heart's command, a voice that speaks
with the pulse of a shoreline,

stems oceans, floods memory.
Here in a surrounded space
we choose song to be who we are,
choose to dance instead of weeping.

When I first heard it I tried to find
how he might have crafted such sorrow;
it felt as if caught from winds, something
coming in across waves' counterpoint,

really a language under language
from beyond walls sea constructs.
On how close or far it is when we sleep
depends the sound an island makes.

Which explains how deep a music's blade
can cut, how a grace note's ornament
sung as the roof's storm beat that night, cracked
open then broke the listening heart.

HAWTHORN CRESCENT

The cotton that fell from her sewing box,
darning something that mattered then
in the seaport suburb, her head bent intent,
her back to the sun, the pot plant,
the piano that rang in sympathy
when she called, there in bay window light,
a cotton thread glistening, thin,
that came loose, unnoticed, falling, falling
through afternoon air when it was August,
and well, it's still falling.

                    Beyond the glass,
a parch of summer grass and a rowan,
lost when they needed some off-road parking
sometime in the time since we've been gone,
in the summers made and broken since.
'Ah sure, but it's none of our business now.'
Borrowed time in the house and its history,
just after the dead moved on, before we did.
Here there's the silver thread hanging in air,
and the grass turning hay under the rowan,
the thread caught in light. She'll notice it later.

SPRING IN THE SUBURBS

After Dame Laura Knight: Spring in St John's Wood,
oil on canvas, c. 1933

When beloved ordinary familiars
demanded attention that day it was because
something in morning light had selected itself
to be saved, a composite essence, a moment
within a place when the season's first suggestion
brought habit out to celebrate the sanctity
of the everyday; quiet weather to preserve
against times when there is no sun, when plants die back,
leafed winds blow across tennis courts, the road empties
of voices and all this is a forgotten thing.
For now at least not so much a view as a way
of life. We grow where we're planted, paint what we see
and hear; this was now and here when the window looked,
she saw, the canvas heard but drew no conclusions
because the place drew conclusions about itself.
Now, when air moves in a certain way, or when
time's right, circumstances still offer suggestions,
because somewhere a window watches, mind's eye sees.

DUTCH SCHOOL

Cardplayers in a Sunlit Room. Pieter de Hooch (1658)

I saw nothing to remark on until the red
of her skirt crossed a Delft day's normality
into mine, domestic unknowns opening wide
the human, its everyday informality.
Suddenly there's an open door, a fold
of time through from another place. Sometimes,
just beyond us but part of us, there's the hold
light has when it's shone aslant spare chequered rooms.
Yes, just like that, reshaping ordinary space.
Softening empty squares, the woman passes
through, touching my time with her indistinct face,
the threshold anticipating their slight glances
up at her, a new shadow entering, while
energy alters like a reawakened smile.

LITTLE DOT HETHERINGTON AT THE OLD BEDFORD

c. 1889. After Walter Sickert

A pennyworth of manufactured Heaven
was what he painted; so easy to believe in
white lace trancing the rapt brown and grey,
immortal for just as long as she was singing
the boy I love is up in the gallery,
beyond performance for them, beguiling
but safe, protected by a blaze of spotlights
and curtained from eviction into their night's
destitute chill seeping anonymous mist
through fluttering Camden gas across lost
courtyards, dimly ticking terraces,
invented sentiment still on their faces,
sinking into the transitory city
again, earthbound and beyond identity.

LITTORAL

1. Beach

A path of sand through sand. Waves purling a blue-grey
rippling dress, lace dishevelled by this westerly,
shoreline the hem of a bay. Winds orchestrate sea.
We were here, but left tide by tide, gradually.

2. *Toward Blue*

It was when a boy skimmed stones
over the murmur at a tide's torn edge
with nowhere to look but here, a time
if it was time at all like a silk cloth
stretching distance, a bright boat
leaving a crease in the bay, water
that slowly healed itself back toward blue.

3. Lemon Barley Water

Still there in the daybreak tang of it, the child,
the trains shunting just beyond the bantam yard,
a shelf, a glass, and the colour of a taste
on mornings when the day promised what nowhere
could deliver, when the air's sleight of hand
tricked hope to believe what might just happen.
And sometimes for a moment it's there again,
a flavour of what's seeded, but never grows.
It was – is – when a sunrise turns grey to gold,
and who knows, with such a light all's possible.
We open like a flower each time. Like children.

4. *Journey into Space*
Science fiction serial, BBC Light Programme, 1953–1958

Encountering the unknown one school at a time,
moving day always a step into the void:
reinvention, beginning again, learning the rules
of the next exclusive club, the eternal new boy, ever
the incomer at the hands of upward mobility.

Each promoted step meant a hostile dialect to unravel.
Children have no option but to follow, and to be so young
was to see migration from familiar worlds as bereavement,
every unaccustomed classroom's inquest betraying
my unacceptable accent, judgement by articulation.

As sound can fall into silence, likewise to speak was to become
solitary, saved when radio's primal light invented
alternative serial empires where we were all foreign
together once a week, and the aerial pulled Ariel
and all his quality out of the night, holding the literal at bay.

While the war of the world ignited round me,
there was I tuning the Bush spaceship to fellow aliens,
peopling galaxies with a mutual language,
my own wavelength listening for the companionship
of voices conjured by space, beings even stranger than I was.

5. *Slow Radio*

At the tone, the time will be that night
when the glass glowed before the sound came,
 the moment recorded itself and outside
there were reeds at the winter's edge,
there was a north wind across marshland.
That night by the lake when the old boat
that would never float again moved slightly
as the waves brushed it through the grasses,
as the lapping seeped through.

And the song when it came, came gradually
from a crackle like a throat clearing,
and when you heard the tone it was 1957,
and it was worth the set's tuning,
the dark whispering across the reedbeds
with the hiss of a distant signal
in place of what was lost,
while the amber-lit wireless smile,
once warmed, stayed constant.

6. *Plane Crash*

Then came a long moment when the child
fell out of the sky, became mortal,
the scream of dying angels silenced,
and the broken blackened wings fluttered
 in pieces down through stillness to earth,
when an instinct dawned that trust was dead,
that age solved nothing, and that
no one had control of anything,
there was no belonging, no centre,
just a continual sense of falling.

RETURN JOURNEY

1. Witch Stone

At low water a witch stone, as waves fall over themselves to land.
You can't remember unless you forget, Samuel said,
and like it or not, recall's under a rock, waiting for Moon's turn,
a two-way mirror, swing-door portal – receiver and transmitter –
the things that we can't quite summon and the things we try to
      erase.

And as often as not it's in shadow, often in the not seen.
Dusk chiaroscuro of a rubble shore; light ebbs and the sand
between crawls and flexes, gives under the feet; this is uncertain
ground, a window in culpable amnesia, the stone itself
a call through a lens to remember while we still have some choice.

And you said you'd be on the threshold ready for when light
      changed.
Well, if this isn't a window – the right time and place – when
      then, where?
If we're to solve it, this as much as any should enable us.
Look into the witch stone as the night comes on and the salt rises.

2. The Pig and Whistle

Chapel Street/Covent Garden, Liverpool, March, 1968

I'll call you Pat then for want of a name
that I met in a dockers' wood warren
of stairs and snugs, and the Belfast steam ship
steaming at the Pier Head, you carrying
Guinness like the grail to your stall past
me as if I wasn't there already,
though we shared the same dark and drank the same
black together, close to the terminal.
Just that and a fragment of my father
that broke off later as he watched me board
toward the next light's start, flying solo
into the angels' share on the Bushmills road.

3. Portstewart
Early Spring, 1968

The search and rescue plane went blind into the dark
and we tensed against storm in a tiny light
against what might brim over the wall's sea edge,
night-long crouching in a back room awaiting
all that torn spring tides at the street's sharp end could throw
our way, what the next day's demand would be.

4. *Improvisation*

Pierre Cochereau plays the organ of Donegall Square
Methodist Church, Belfast. Sunday March 10, 1968

Church at eight-thirty,
air still warm from the faithful,
and Cochereau plays,

improvises us,
extemporises on hymns,
makes our known songs new,

takes the worn, loved notes,
then from imagination
finds fresh ways to hear.

'Simple joy, simple sadness'
changed to something astounding,
a point of view

never considered,
entrenched airs given such strange
possibilities,

a flight of music
that never has been before
or will be again.

Learnt hymns are one thing
but what he's proposing here,
oh, quite another.

5. *Interval*

Photograph of the three of us
there, a Lough Beg springtime Sunday,
a pause archived out of context,
all smiles for the Instamatic.

You'd never know to look at us,
neither did we, scheduled to be
elsewhere, driving the Fiat off
to the far end of a grey lane.

How we came here, what happened next,
the hinterland of circumstance,
who knows? But at our backs, across
water, black trees, white blank sky.

6. *All Hallows' Eve*

Doors closing one by one,
diseased by division, denial.
We're so many ragged ghosts,
hollow as infected jack-o'-lanterns

in cramped windows, nowhere
to go because going anywhere
is not an option. We celebrate
alone the ceremony of fear.

At night we dream space,
pearl air over wide
peninsulas, arcs of light,
opalescent, of infinite height,

places where nothing
needs saying, more sky
than we'll ever need.
We dream like children,

but wake to whatever it is
crawling dark up the path
to the door. Sleep again.
When it knocks, don't answer.

7. *Shadow*

Shadow stumbles, lifts herself,
encouraged by light walks tall.

Queen of the dark side and chilled,
she follows, melts, vanishes,

moving silently on through
shouting worlds. You'd never know.

A backroom girl, she reflects
on the day, works flexible

hours, interprets what she sees,
only comes home on moonless nights,

the shut door of a closed eye,
the echoless rooms of dark,

does her best work behind our backs,
but then sometimes predicts us.

She has no need of boasting,
knows soon she'll grow to an eclipse.

8. Song for Mina

Foolhardy girl from border land,
they told you I was ill-advised,
and that my coming could kill you.
Tiny indomitable girl.

Just as if it wasn't enough
to marry His Majesty's Navy.
Then my coming, to prove to them
another stranger couldn't hurt you.

Deep inside, engraved in spirit,
the part they couldn't change, a past.
I'll spell his name my way she said,
knowing she'd survive through that.

Border girl with a fever-hurt
heart and broken lungs, no wonder –
biting a towel to swallow
your blood-letting screams, anything

to hide my birth murdering you,
to mock their mocking, the Irish
they watched and wanted to see fail,
flame of unbroken Monaghan girl –

no wonder your love could be fierce,
no wonder nothing was too good
for the child everyone feared for
but you and your emerald fire.

Well, you kept your voice for Ireland,
made the red stain that became me,
and we came through, right enough, so
I'll sing it for the two of us now.

9. *An Old Violin*

Strings creaked, but then, archived from deep in it,
a witness that had held its tongue a lifetime,
as fingers remembered something long unsung
and forbidden, brought from the instinct of it,
tides' voice coming past the estuary's end.
It'll be full of sea's horizons by now,
he said, *such sadness pent up and saved so long,*
it would have learnt to sing itself anyway.

And then years later when I walked down the lane
to the waterside, just about halfway
along – there, where light seems to modulate, tense
with the river's closeness – I could hear the song,
its exile's rebel refrain, as when he played,
just as he said, singing in tides' flow, time's shift.

PETRICHOR

We're here again in an ancient porch
listening to the daylight's dissolve.
After all the endured weeks of heat,
here's sheer summer rain sibilating.
The evening turns liquid. Petrichor,
the smell of parched earth drinking.

Air exhales time with a slow hiss,
the acoustic garden answering,
each leaf surface its own dialect,
a community of foliage,
the particular and assorted
now a single species, all colours
sipping the soak of warm rain as one,
the shared scent, democracy of growth.

GRIME'S GRAVES
Norfolk

Wide skies across The Brecks and straight roads
enough to tease boy racers to death.
We walked through this way to Walsingham
you once told me. All of us pilgrims.

These straight roads, big skies hold sermons
for seekers, such ready metaphors,
so much air to plunge through, so much space
with nothing in it but a raptor

poised on thermals scouring God's flat earth,
a rusted van and a kill in couch grass,
a broken Skoda, *Police Aware*,
still warm under flinty pock-marked cloud.

HANDWRITTEN

The cherry tree in evening light,
amber light through Bushmills.

Paper's fragility. Ink
fading. I can picture you

sitting there at the table
by the garden window.

It's where you used to write, where
you filled all those red Silvines.

Two glasses of Black Bush.
The sound of you again. I read,

you pour into the room.
Leafing through, I listen.

The ink dries, the voice fades,
the page turns, a door.

But I go on hearing it,
because though this was then,

sounds we made still make us,
the grain of particulars.

APPLE WOOD

John Fuller, Wood Carver

Here's a face emerging, released from beneath bark,
your energy held in it, manifest. It flows
under my fingers now, following the line of yours.
I bite the fresh fruit for the memory of you,

smell the tang of reborn wood-flesh savouring air,
the sweet blood from the trunk's artery your gold ore,
explaining change to the tree, your sweet alchemy,
conceiving a new being at the blade's sharp kiss.

Intimate as love, the palpable idea of you
braille-tactile, your voice transmitting murmurings
that whispered up to you as grain's flow suggested
itself, turning pliable, birthing shapes to light.

I saw you become part of the wood, your engraved face
matching it gnarl for knot as the rings grew round you
in the timber henge yard, I saw you out-staring
your celtic sea, looking for ways to etch a wave.

Now I loosen stacked words from the page's lumber,
try to shape a poem as tangible as you,
autumn's apples whipped by winds from beyond Skomer,
these splinters of rain on my face chipped from darkness.

FISHERMAN

Aghast when the gales blew,
the twirl, eddy, how the trees
stared back at the wind,
he was always alive to the day,

how the river leafed under
light in late October
when the line went slack
and there was nothing.

All the time the same place
on the bank, proprietorial
he was, in that corner there
under the willow. Morning

wouldn't lighten till he came,
sun or storm, always alive
to the day, and the day
hasn't dawned the same since,

fish won't rise as they did
for him, when their death
was love given him, his death
the life he gave them back.

DEAUVILLE

i.m. Elizabeth Finn, Painter

Sunday morning, sea rumouring
a tide's turn. I would know this light
anywhere, blue, gold murmuring,
your laughter flying like a kite.
It's a music to circumvent
mortality, jazz that's timeless,
transmuting a doubt's last fragment,
painting this song as a witness
to ignite things we never knew
had dimmed here, tuned to now, always
pure-sharp as the present tense, through
air gilded by the sand-bright days,
a diamond forever on
the boardwalk in Calvados sun.

ON THE AIR

1. A Candle for Piers Plowright
   The Return of the Hunters, also known as *The Hunters in the Snow*.
   Oil-on-wood, 1565. Pieter Brueghel the Elder

People were skating when the elder Brueghel
sent his men and dogs homeward across snow,
and evening's first fluttering candle
lit a valley window somewhere below
them, its glow igniting the dusk, a thrill
of fire beneath the mountain, a known light
hung on darkness, owning the sacred skill
to take thought on to where a prayer might
transcend the loneliest fragile gleam,
blaze up into night and set it apart
from other meanings. Or so it would seem
from the spreading scintillas candles start.
A wished-on flame can shape walls' winter frieze
to benediction. And the traveller sees.

2. At the Window
  New End Square, Hampstead
  After Jimmy Yancey

Well Walk, the place's clock printing the hour,
ticking Keats, Keats, and somewhere in its midst
faint sounds of Jimmy's *White Sox Stomp* (1943)
from the house with the rocking horse
across the way, sundial shadows timing
leaf, brick dust and me, layered parts
of this particular September day.

Someone passes and pauses, smiles.
We are both ghosts, as much here as anywhere,
time meeting itself coming back, belonging
to a song I once knew, late sun's echoed greeting
from Chicago, 12-bars on a hiss of shellac,
and *At the Window*, the ghost of a horse nodding
to Yancey. Music is more than its sound.

3. *Written in Stone*

Rooks calling as the evening comes.
Over two fields, there's the blue energy of sea and sky.
Here, the orchard wall made around 1820
framing variations on a green song.

Dry stones, and each a decision, a judgement,
as tree planters work for futures beyond them,
a fixed music under changes of air and light,
lightness and weight, fencing this quickening,

increasing through stanzas to a poem,
word by word, an intention published, blended
from a chaos of rubble to harmony,
tuned from land rabble to community,

a choir of voices grown from local earth,
this pattern of shapes locked by the logic of tessellation
into euphony, designed against Time, weather,
incursion, willed by a requirement for enclosure,

and held together by complementary differences
in a mutually pragmatic configuration,
learning association as disparate particles,
learning society as birds roost in their wood.

The rooks fade from clamour to silent parliament,
Pipistrelles' invisible sound
scans the lane's dusk. On the edge of awareness,
an unwritten nameless man, job done, home-bound.

4. Chestnut Tree

John Donne: *Hymne to God my God, in my sicknesse*
i.m. P.P.

A chair by a bed. But mostly a window full of tree,
the chestnut tree broadcasting each evening down the line:
I'm looking at it now, it's become a friend. I saw it
clearly like the best radio, full of its summer
through your commentary, light measuring time, observation
from behind the glass finding the poem in it and then
painting it all wirelessly, the sum of its parts melded.
All those weeks, the dial set to you and the chestnut tree,
and it was an unmissable programme, an appointment
to listen until you went off the air, into the air.

You read Donne: *I shall be made thy musique; As I come
I tune the Instrument here at the dore.* This is transmission,
frequency and wavelength, the chestnut rehearsing with you,
and still there through its seasons, a bell ringing in my head
because you made it a story, the idea of it.
Your precise articulation writes itself on new time,
so through every change you're there in the instrument tuned,
each chestnut tree recreating your pictures in the mind,
imagination turning the unseen into memory,
which was the trick you always did, which is what you still do.

5. Slant

On a rooftop level with trees.
There's not a breath and not a leaf
in the whole beech city stirring,
not a wing and not a prayer
moving air. It's that time of day
of them all when walls come down,
divides fall, as though I could turn,
speak to you, knowing if ever
we were, then now we're together,
 but knowing to look's to lose it
in the shock of a moment's glimpse.
Too much light for it to be held,
when what flashes on the pure edge
becomes a ripened entity
and loses itself in telling,
how what happens becomes a fact
that still requires explanation.

6. Formby Beach

Migrant winds chorusing through the marram grass,
an aeolian harp rooted for airplay,
an air for setting the poem the wildfowl
write with their V, their chanting high above dunes
answering the change that adopts them across
the liminal from imagined curves of earth.

Their call emerges from the wash and hum of
transmissions between here and where gales strum on
other grasses. Coast is a border crossing.
The marram duets, but it doesn't translate
the delta flock's shout, carving their arrival
in sky, tipped by a pivot of atmosphere,

here because of a trigger that fires in them
the urgency of leaving, a promised space.
The dunes go on composing new harmonies,
hissing through winter, their sand tide reshaping
in harmony with the next incoming storm.
Marram grass sings. Changing light chases the fade.

RIVERING

1. Shoreline

He comes up from the shoreline each night, through
stunted Elders, past the broken buildings.
Salt's in his step, a deck's shift in his walk.
He came up from the river again last night.
Though he didn't knock, we knew he was there.

Along the wharf, warehouses die slowly.
Buddleia's advanced guard insinuates
change root by root, invades defeated brick
one repossession at a time. River's edge
though, that's where you really see time, ebb tide.

Rippling light along an oblique timeline
of waves chasing shores with nowhere to run,
estuaries' arms wide for prodigal seas.
Each breaker a line and each rock that ends
it a rhyme, every tide a new poem.

2. Docking

He is moving down river, morning light.
What else moves on the wind? Only the gulls,
only rusted fragments along old wharves.
Gulls on the broken quays, picking at crumbs
fallen from ships gone to the breaker's yard.

Coming in towards a city sunrise,
nineteen fifty nine, a Canadian
Pacific is docking today. Today,
the Empress of England, her steel tonnage
floating featherlike on dawn's horizon.

Tugs fuss, the arms of the dock enfold her.
On deck, a girl watches the new light rise,
then time ebbs again, memory sends waves
lapping, and a wash across the river
flounders on sea walls. Watch as water leaves,

memory filling these empty seascapes,
scrap metal-mangled quays where lives landed,
the glory age when the river flowed gold,
held in the harbour's conch shell acoustic.
Recalled light, time past skims like a stone.

3. *Flow*

Every stone's a photograph in shoreline's
gallery, likenesses on jaundiced sand.
It's where the drowned come when they become tired
of drowning, each small rock its own meaning.
Shelve them as keepsakes of what they were.

A wisp of seaweed clings to a pebble,
lank hair on a found face shifting slowly
in the inhale, exhale at the tide mark.
One of the river's chosen, who chose it.
The gift it offers of flowing away.

Hinterlands can be tribal, you learn
the hard way: a tone of voice, you learn that
in the pursuit of belonging, voices
of place, the river's many languages,
the syntax of immigration.

A child builds castle walls, ramparts from a ridge
of pebbles against the next tide. As seas
rise, people submerge one by one, slowly
but for their heads like stones, dressed in these wisps
of weed, belonging where they are at last.

4. *Here*

Tidal but still. Reflections.
Sand imitates water, water sand.
Gulls stab at themselves.

Nowhere to go but here
but here is where
the moment happens,

always happens. Inside
the radio is playing
Out of Time, but here

the river sings *Who*
Knows Where the Time Goes,
and I can see where it goes

from here downstream out
to what's always been ebbing,
always coming home.

MOONSTONE

For Phoebe, born 15 June, 2014,
and for Zoe, Jemma and Jo

I brought you a moonstone to chime
with your luminous morning, your pure
light, the ancient gift carried by time.
That an essence so bequeathed can endure
you have the right to expect
world to acknowledge and to respect.
Daughters of daughters, each beginning
in a beginning, you inherit
a torch while giving fresh meaning
to being in the way you declare it.
Here's a fruit transferred, flowering anew
in the spirit that flows today through you.
You are the sole creator of the song you sing,
but radiance is also a transmitted thing.

PLANTED

After Homer: The Odyssey, Book XXIV

And then coming home through patterns of streets
to that remembered lost childhood's garden,
dreaming, he found his father still living,
working in the same place, the very place
in spite of all.
             So they found each other
through patterns of roots – pear, apple, fig, vine –
remnants of a recollected orchard.

PYRACANTHA

There was the frost, light fighting to rise
in the garden, there was a blackbird
and blood berries: the pyracantha,
bred to feed winter through fire thorns
spilling red juice over frozen wings.

POEM AT THE END OF A YEAR

Crosby Beach. After Antony Gormley

It's just the sort of sky you know they came here for,
these with iron hearts aspiring to be melted.

Living hands haunting this beach, the loving touch
of flesh, reaching out of arms, homecoming's embrace,

expectation's relief, fulfilment of hope against fear.
It's what this shore was shaped for, waiting and watching,

so throw us a line, sunset, as you sink; who knows,
we may yet lead each other to another place.

EVENING

After Marilynne Robinson

Speak it with three syllables:
the day is being smoothed,
evening itself to darkness.

Don't draw the curtain
or switch on the light.
Let it all slowly change

till out and in are equal.
Darkness like water:
let the room fill gradually,

imperceptibly, leaving us
deep, submerged in its calm,
its even, total sea.

THE NEXT BIG THING

One day soon – in the next two
million years – Betelgeuse
will explode. Look at it now
with its Plantagenet light
pulsing red on Orion's
shoulder, preparing to die.
The ignition of a light
half the size of a solar
system in anechoic
dark, what kind of messiah
will that hatch? I prepare myself.
Camera set on tripod,
Flask, telescope, sacred texts
always there at the ready –
it won't catch me out this time:
divinities choose their moment,
and the readiness is all.
Meanwhile, to while away sun,
which blinds out all the real things,
I stare into the dark cracks
between, looking out for proof
spilled from dead stars and lost gods
in the deep space below me.

LIFT OFF

After 'Le Saut dans le Vide.' Yves Klein, 1960

Here's the plan (subject to change).
It will be from this window,
over an imagined spring
and across the greening park.

Below, the bus stop will be
awaiting the next coming
of the eighty six to town.
It won't come. It won't matter.

Neither will the empty train
concern itself that no one
will be travelling today
except the man who lifts off,

intent on his trajectory.
The sky will be blue of course:
the trick is in the timing,
to recognise the right light.

At that moment a boy
will pass on a mountain bike,
practising a wheelie, as if
trying his hardest to fly.

NOTES

Spring in the Suburbs
Spring in St John's Wood, oil on canvas, c. 1933 by Dame Laura Knight. Walker Art Gallery, Liverpool.

Dutch School
Cardplayers in a Sunlit Room, Pieter de Hooch (1658). The painting is in the Royal Collection at Windsor Castle.

Little Dot Hetherington at The Old Bedford
The painter Walter Sickert (1860–1942) was drawn to theatrical and music hall subjects all his life, and painted the artists, audience and internal architecture of The Bedford Music Hall in Camden Town in particular on a number of occasions, both before and after its rebuilding following a fire in the late 1890s. The subject of this poem comes from two of his paintings: 'Little Dot Hetherington at the Bedford Music Hall', (The Picture Art Collection) painted in 1888–89, and 'Gallery of the Old Bedford' (Walker Art Gallery, Liverpool), painted in 1894–95. Subsequent paintings of 'The New Bedford' were created in 1907–8 and 1914–15.

Journey into Space
This BBC radio science fiction serial was translated into 17 languages and broadcast globally during its 5-year span. In British radio history it is notable in that it was the last evening programme of its era to attract an audience larger than the one watching television at the time.

Plane Crash
As a six year-old child, I was present at the Farnborough Air Show disaster of 1952, and witnessed a DH110 jet disintegrate, killing the pilot and observer, and 29 spectators in the crowd.

Return Journey

During 1968, I spent some months in Belfast and Portstewart in Northern Ireland touring with a theatre in education company, when the Province was on the brink of 'The Troubles.' During that time, I was able to explore some of the terrain in which my mother grew up, and where my parents met during the Second World War.

Witch Stone

'Witch Stones' can be any type of stone that has a natural hole through it. Some consider Witch Stones to be sacred objects. They have been called by many names over the centuries including Hag Stones, Adder Stones, Snake Eggs, Hex Stones, Fairy Stones, Holy Stones, Holeys, and Eye Stones. There is a belief held in some cultures that other worlds may be glimpsed by looking through them. In line 2, 'Samuel' refers to Samuel Beckett, and a comment he made about memory in an essay on Proust.

Improvisation

Pierre Cochereau (1924–1984), was the organist of Notre Dame Cathedral in Paris from 1955 until his death. On March 10, 1968, he gave a recital at Donegall Square Methodist Church, Belfast; he finished the performance with one of the improvisations for which he was famous, taking as his text the hymn tunes, *St. Columba* and *Duke Street*, a twenty-minute tour de force which a local critic called 'a miracle of inventiveness.' The church building subsequently fell into disuse during The Troubles, when bombings in central Belfast drove its congregation away to suburban churches. but the listed façade was later incorporated into a new building housing the head office of the Ulster Bank. The line which begins stanza 4, 'Simple joy, simple sadness', references Kingsley Amis's poem, 'Farewell Blues', first published in the *New Statesman* (30 March 1979), in which Amis laments jazz's 'simple joy and simple sadness', replaced by 'keyless, barless' noise.

Grime's Graves
A Neolithic flint mining complex in Norfolk, seven miles north-west of Thetford off the A134.

On the Air
This sequence is in memory of the BBC radio features producer, Piers Plowright, who died in July, 2021.

A Candle for Piers Plowright
Based on *The Return of the Hunters*, also known as *The Hunters in the Snow*. Oil-on-wood, 1565. Pieter Brueghel the Elder. Kunsthistorisches Museum, Vienna.

Poem at the End of a Year
Crosby Beach, Merseyside is the home of *Another Place*, a work by Sir Antony Gormley consisting of 100 cast iron figures facing towards the sea.

Evening
Suggested by a passage in Marilynne Robinson's novel, *Housekeeping*.

Lift Off (April)
Le Saut dans le vide (Leap into the Void) is a photomontage by Harry Shunk and Janos Kender of a performance by Yves Klein at Rue Gentil-Bernard, Fontenay-aux-Roses in October 1960. The trick photograph shows Klein jumping off a wall, arms outstretched, as if projecting himself towards the sky.